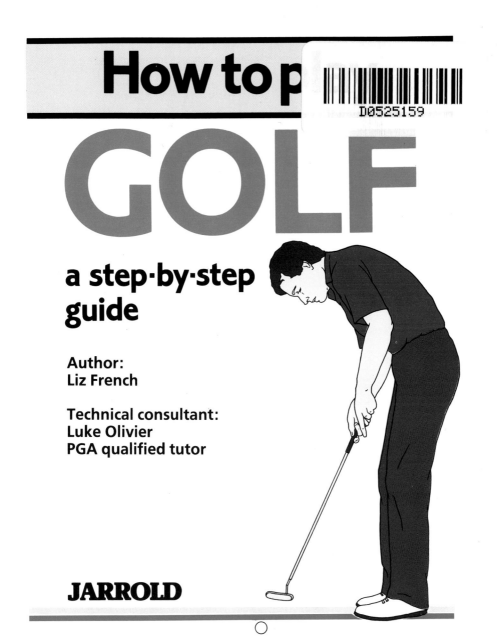

How to p[lay]

GOLF

a step·by·step guide

Author:
Liz French

Technical consultant:
Luke Olivier
PGA qualified tutor

JARROLD

D0525159

Other sports covered in this series are:

AMERICAN FOOTBALL	**SAILING A DINGHY**
BADMINTON	**SNOOKER**
BASKETBALL	**SOCCER**
BOWLS	**SQUASH**
COARSE FISHING	**SWIMMING**
CRICKET	**TABLE TENNIS**
CROQUET	**TENNIS**
GET FIT FOR SPORT	**WINDSURFING**
HOCKEY	

How to play GOLF
ISBN 0-7117-0502-X

Text © Liz French 1990
This edition © Jarrold Publishing 1990
Illustrations by Malcolm Ryan

First published 1990
Reprinted 1992, 1994

Designed and produced by
Parke Sutton Limited, Norwich
for Jarrold Publishing, Norwich
Printed in Great Britain 3/94

Contents

Introduction

Golf is one of the most popular games in the world — and with good reason. It can be enjoyed by beginners as much as by more experienced players, and by all age groups. It challenges the intellect as much as the physique. It can be frustrating, fickle and addictive. It is also immensely enjoyable.

Wherever you live, there is bound to be a golf course nearby. Whilst it is true that golf is not the cheapest of sports to take up, it is certainly not necessary to spend enormous amounts on equipment: a carefully chosen second-hand half set of clubs will meet your needs for some time. The social aspects of golf are also an attractive feature of the game for many players: clubs hold regular tournaments and medal competitions and there are plenty of opportunities for new friendships.

As a beginner, your main task is to master the movements that will give you a powerful and dependable swing. This book will take you through the fundamental principles. It will also acquaint you with the basic etiquette, terminology and rules of the game and give you some ideas for practising and problem solving. Taking a few lessons with a golf professional is highly recommended when you are new to the game. It is much harder to correct bad habits later. You can also learn a great deal from observing more experienced players, so do get out on the course and watch any matches you can.

Golf is, above all, a game for enjoyment, and as you progress and improve your game, you will find this fascinating sport a source of increasing and lasting pleasure.

COURSE AND EQUIPMENT

The Course

A standard full course consists of 18 'holes'. A hole is the playing area between and including the teeing ground and its green where the hole itself is located. Holes vary in length from about 100-600yds (90-550m) and include a number of features and obstacles such as rough ground, areas of water and bunkers. The illustrations shown here are of one typical hole.

When playing at a particular course, ask if there is a 'course planner' available. This will illustrate the features and measurements of each hole on the course and will help you decide which clubs to play (see pages 8-9 and 29).

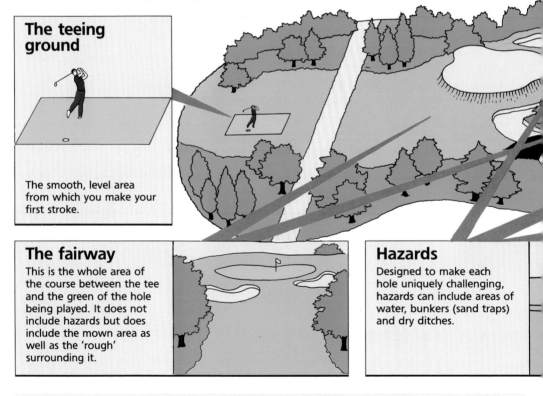

The teeing ground

The smooth, level area from which you make your first stroke.

The fairway

This is the whole area of the course between the tee and the green of the hole being played. It does not include hazards but does include the mown area as well as the 'rough' surrounding it.

Hazards

Designed to make each hole uniquely challenging, hazards can include areas of water, bunkers (sand traps) and dry ditches.

The aim of the game

Using a variety of clubs, you hit the ball into each hole in succession, taking the lowest possible number of strokes. You can compete individually or in pairs. There are two basic forms of competition play — match play and stroke play. Basically, in match play the side or individual winning the most holes wins the match. In stroke play, the winner is the player who finishes the course in the fewest strokes.

The green

The area of carefully prepared grass in which the hole itself is located.

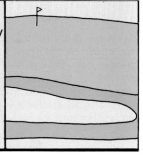

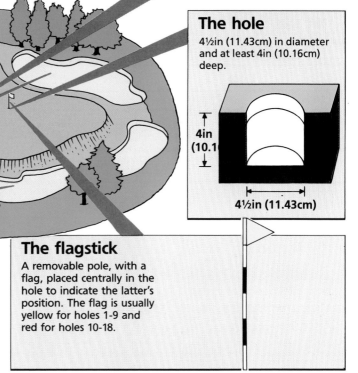

The hole

4½in (11.43cm) in diameter and at least 4in (10.16cm) deep.

4in (10.1...)

4½in (11.43cm)

The flagstick

A removable pole, with a flag, placed centrally in the hole to indicate the latter's position. The flag is usually yellow for holes 1-9 and red for holes 10-18.

The Clubs

There are three basic types of club: woods, irons and putters. The angle of the face and the length of the shaft vary according to the kind of shot a club is designed to play. The steeper the angle of the face, the higher the trajectory of the shot. This angle is known as the 'loft' of the club.

You can use a maximum of 14 clubs during a round. You will want to acquire your own clubs, and advice on how to choose them will be found on page 10.

Wood	Iron	Putter

Woods

A wood has a head of wood, plastic or light metal that is fairly wide from front to back. It is used for long shots. Woods are numbered from 1 (the 'driver') to 5, with loft factors ranging from 12° to 28°. Numbers 2 and 4 woods, however, are very rarely used nowadays.

Woods	Loft factor
No 1	12°
No 2	16°
No 3	20°
No 4	24°
No 5	28°

Irons

Irons are used for the majority of shots on the fairway. An iron has a head that is relatively narrow from front to back, usually made of steel. The shaft is shorter than that of a wood. Irons are numbered from 1 to 9, plus the putting wedge and sand-iron. In a matched set, the low numbered clubs have the least amount of loft and the longest shafts. Use these for long, low shots. The high numbered, short-shafted clubs are used for short, high shots.

W   8   5   3   2

Irons	Loft factor		
1-iron	14°	6-iron	34°
2-iron	18°	7-iron	38°
3-iron	22°	8-iron	42°
4-iron	26°	9-iron	46°
5-iron	30°	Pitching wedge	52°
		Sand-iron	58°

Putters

Putters are made in a variety of shapes and the type you select is purely a matter of personal choice. As its name suggests, the putter is used to play the ball once it is on the putting green.

Shaft length

As the clubs go down in number and loft factor, so the shafts are lengthened by ½in (1.27cm) per club. Together with the decreasing loft, this makes the ball travel a longer distance—around 10-12 yds (9-11m) more for each club. (See also page 29).

Choosing Your Clubs

Ask an expert

Don't be tempted to order a set of clubs from a department store or by mail order — it will be a false economy. Your age, sex, height and strength all need to be taken into account, and it is best to go to a qualified professional who will know which kind of clubs will suit you best.

A half set

You don't need a full set to begin with. Ideally, aim to start with a number 3 and a number 5 wood, 4-, 6- and 8-irons, a pitching wedge or sand-iron and a putter.

When choosing clubs, you should check these points:

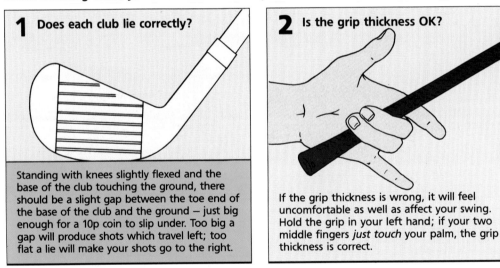

1 **Does each club lie correctly?**

Standing with knees slightly flexed and the base of the club touching the ground, there should be a slight gap between the toe end of the base of the club and the ground — just big enough for a 10p coin to slip under. Too big a gap will produce shots which travel left; too flat a lie will make your shots go to the right.

2 **Is the grip thickness OK?**

If the grip thickness is wrong, it will feel uncomfortable as well as affect your swing. Hold the grip in your left hand; if your two middle fingers *just touch* your palm, the grip thickness is correct.

3 **Is the shaft flex correct?**

Golf club shafts come in various flexes, from very stiff to very flexible and this affects the way a club plays. You can choose from L, ladies; A, active; R, regular or S, stiff. For most beginners an L or A flex is usually the best choice.

The Ball

The ball is made of rubber with a plastic outer surface that is dimpled to improve the accuracy and distance of flight.

Size

The old British ball with a diameter of 1.62in (4.11cm) has now disappeared in favour of its larger American counterpart which is 1.68in (4.27cm) in diameter. Make sure, if you are buying secondhand balls, that they are the larger size.

Markings

Balls are marked with the manufacturer's logo and a number for easy identification during matches. It is usual to check on the first tee that every player has an easily identifiable ball.

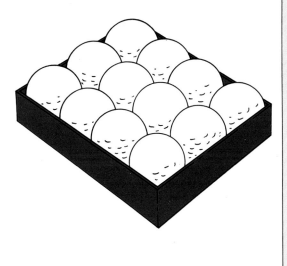

Type

There are two types of ball:

Wound balls

These have elastic tightly wound around a central core. They can be covered in a material called surlyn, which is tougher and resists damage, or in balata, which is softer but cuts more easily. The latter type gives more backspin and is favoured by professionals.

Solid balls

These are made from a solid rubber core with a tough plastic coating and are very durable. They are also cheaper than wound balls and ideal for beginners.

Dress and Accessories

Dress

There are golf fashions as in all sports, but as a general rule aim to be casual but not scruffy! Men often need a jacket and tie for the clubhouse, but for playing many opt for a 'V' necked sweater and short-sleeved shirt worn with casual trousers – not shorts or jeans. Women can wear skirts or tailored trousers.

Shoes

There are no strict rules here – although, naturally, heels are not allowed – but since you'll be walking several miles during a round of golf, a good pair of golf shoes is an extremely good investment. The soles have either spikes or small rubber pimples for grip. After use, do remember to clean them off and, if conditions have been wet, dry them slowly and always remove spiked shoes before entering the clubhouse.

Gloves

Many players wear a leather glove on their left hand to avoid the discomfort of friction which can occur. If you choose to wear one, make sure it fits snugly but not too tightly.

Accessories

A glance through the advertisements in any golfing magazine or a browse round the pro-shop reveals a baffling range of accessories for the golfer. Here are a few particularly useful ones.

Bags

You can choose from an enormous variety of sizes, weights and materials — a light-weight nylon type is a good choice for beginners. You can also hire or buy a trolley to wheel your clubs around.

Tees

You can play the first stroke of any hole off a tee (it's easier than playing off the ground) and can buy wooden or plastic ones of different lengths.

Ball marker

When on the green, your ball may sometimes obstruct the path of your partner's. In this case, you may pick it up and mark the spot with this useful little gadget.

Pitch mark repairer

If your ball causes a dent in the green, this useful tool repairs the damage.

Umbrella

A large golfing umbrella is often a very useful accessory. After use, open it up and let it dry in a warm atmosphere.

ETIQUETTE AND RULES

Etiquette

Etiquette on the golf course is of great importance and is largely a matter of consideration for others and preservation of the course. Not knowing the rules can cause embarrassment and other golfers will certainly respect you for observing these basic courtesies, which make the game more enjoyable for everyone.

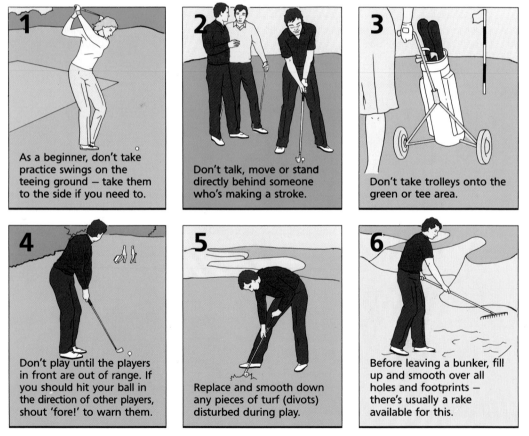

1 As a beginner, don't take practice swings on the teeing ground — take them to the side if you need to.

2 Don't talk, move or stand directly behind someone who's making a stroke.

3 Don't take trolleys onto the green or tee area.

4 Don't play until the players in front are out of range. If you should hit your ball in the direction of other players, shout 'fore!' to warn them.

5 Replace and smooth down any pieces of turf (divots) disturbed during play.

6 Before leaving a bunker, fill up and smooth over all holes and footprints — there's usually a rake available for this.

7

If you have lost a ball, let oncoming matches through – don't hunt for five minutes before doing so! In fact, you should let others through if for *any* reason you are delayed or have to play slowly.

8

Do let people you have invited through get out of range before continuing with your own game.

9

Be especially careful to repair any damage to the green. Watch for, and tidy up, damage from shoe spikes, and handle the flagstick carefully to avoid damaging the edge of the hole.

10

Don't lean on your putter, particularly when removing the ball from the hole – it could damage the green.

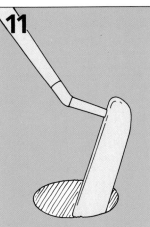

11

Don't flick the ball out of the hole with your putter.

12

In the interests of all, you should play without delay. It is especially important to leave the green as soon as your last player has holed out – you can fill out your score cards on the next tee.

General Rules

There are 34 listed rules in golf, with numerous clauses and variations, and it is well worth getting yourself a copy of the official rules booklet, available (usually free) from most clubs. However, if you work on the general principle of 'play the ball where it lies', you will not go far wrong. Here, some of the rules and procedures most relevant to beginners are highlighted.

NOTE: Some rules vary for stroke and match play, particularly where penalties are incurred — check your rule book.

GENERAL POINTS

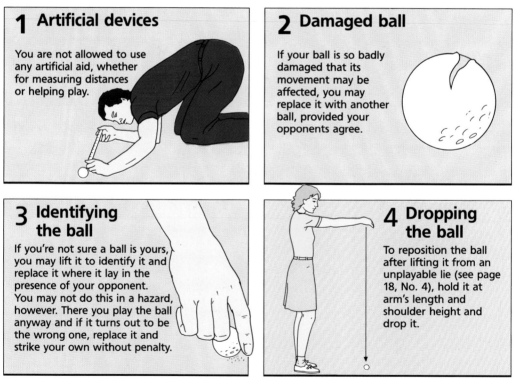

1 Artificial devices

You are not allowed to use any artificial aid, whether for measuring distances or helping play.

2 Damaged ball

If your ball is so badly damaged that its movement may be affected, you may replace it with another ball, provided your opponents agree.

3 Identifying the ball

If you're not sure a ball is yours, you may lift it to identify it and replace it where it lay in the presence of your opponent. You may not do this in a hazard, however. There you play the ball anyway and if it turns out to be the wrong one, replace it and strike your own without penalty.

4 Dropping the ball

To reposition the ball after lifting it from an unplayable lie (see page 18, No. 4), hold it at arm's length and shoulder height and drop it.

STARTING THE GAME

1 Order of play

In tournaments, the club committee organises a draw to determine order of play. In friendly matches, toss a coin. Subsequently, the side winning the hole decides who plays first at the next teeing ground. This is known as the 'honour'.

2 First ball

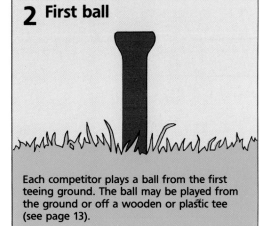

Each competitor plays a ball from the first teeing ground. The ball may be played from the ground or off a wooden or plastic tee (see page 13).

3 Outside the teeing ground

You may stand outside the teeing ground to play your first stroke, but your ball must be within it.

4 Ball off the tee

If your ball falls or is knocked off the tee before you've played, you may replace it. If a stroke has been played, however, it is counted.

PROCEDURE THROUGH THE FAIRWAY

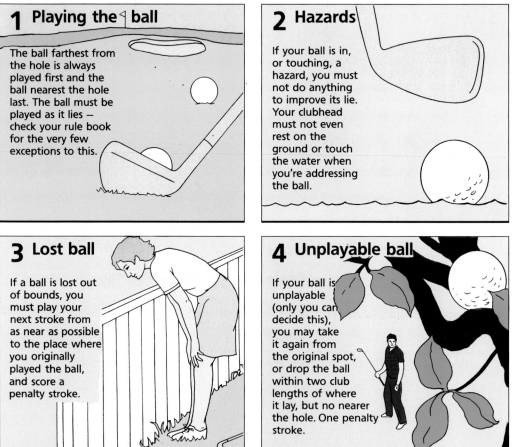

1 Playing the ball

The ball farthest from the hole is always played first and the ball nearest the hole last. The ball must be played as it lies — check your rule book for the very few exceptions to this.

2 Hazards

If your ball is in, or touching, a hazard, you must not do anything to improve its lie. Your clubhead must not even rest on the ground or touch the water when you're addressing the ball.

3 Lost ball

If a ball is lost out of bounds, you must play your next stroke from as near as possible to the place where you originally played the ball, and score a penalty stroke.

4 Unplayable ball

If your ball is unplayable (only you can decide this), you may take it again from the original spot, or drop the ball within two club lengths of where it lay, but no nearer the hole. One penalty stroke.

5 Wrong ball

If you play the wrong ball, except in a hazard (see page 16, No. 3), you incur two penalty strokes.

PROCEDURE ON THE PUTTING GREEN

1 Line of the putt

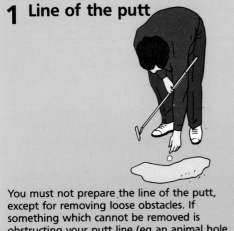

You must not prepare the line of the putt, except for removing loose obstacles. If something which cannot be removed is obstructing your putt line (eg an animal hole or a puddle), you may lift the ball and place it down again, but no nearer the hole.

2 The flagstick

You may have the flagstick held up or removed to indicate the hole before you play your stroke. If your ball hits the flagstick or the person holding it, you incur two penalty strokes.

What's Your Handicap?

The handicapping system allows players of different skill levels to compete on level terms. Your handicap is based on the number of strokes by which you normally exceed the rating (par) for the course. The maximum handicap is 28 for a man and 36 for a woman.

You will probably need a handicap if you want to join the club. The usual requirement is to play three rounds with a club member marking your score against the standard scratch score for the course. Once you have a handicap you can participate in the medal competitions run by your club, and if your scores improve, your handicap will be reduced by the handicap committee.

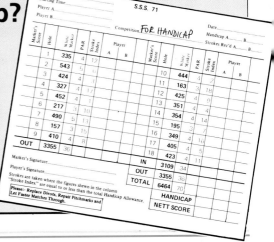

Key Number..................
Starting Time..................
Player A..................
Player B..................

S.S.S. 71

Competition FOR HANDICAP

Date..................
Handicap A.......... B..........
Strokes Rec'd A.......... B..........

Marker's Score	Hole	White Marker	PAR	Stroke Index	Player A	Player B	Marker's Score	Hole	White Marker	PAR	Stroke Index	Player A	Player B
	1	335	4	12				10	444	4	2		
	2	543	5					11	163	3	18		
	3	424	4					12	425	4	9		
	4	327	4	17				13	351	4			
	5	452	4					14	354	4	14		
	6	217	3	10				15	195	3			
	7	490	5	13				16	349	4	10		
	8	157	3	16				17	405	4	5		
	9	410	4	8				18	423	4	11		
OUT		3355	36				IN		3109	34			
							OUT		3355	36			
							TOTAL		6464	70			

Marker's Signature..................

Player's Signature..................

Strokes are taken where the figures shewn in the column "Stroke Index" are equal to or less than the total Handicap Allowance.

Please: Replace Divots, Repair Pitchmarks and Let Faster Matches Through.

HANDICAP

NETT SCORE

THE SWING

In this section the different elements of the swing are analysed in turn. If this seems daunting at first, don't be put off. Remember that the swing is in fact one fluid movement. When you are actually out there playing, the best advice is to relax and not to try too hard. No two players ever strike the ball exactly the same way, and there are some very successful unorthodox swings in the game! Later in the book you will find instructions for varying this basic swing for specific shots and situations.

Addressing the Ball

Addressing the ball correctly is as vital as the swing itself, and you need to consider five factors: aim, grip, ball position, stance and body alignment, and posture. All the instructions given here are for a right-handed player – reverse them as appropriate if you are left-handed.

Aim

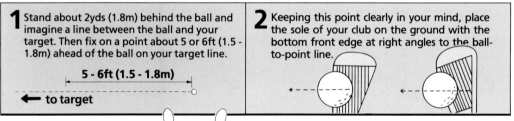

1 Stand about 2yds (1.8m) behind the ball and imagine a line between the ball and your target. Then fix on a point about 5 or 6ft (1.5 - 1.8m) ahead of the ball on your target line.

5 - 6ft (1.5 - 1.8m)

← to target

2 Keeping this point clearly in your mind, place the sole of your club on the ground with the bottom front edge at right angles to the ball-to-point line.

Grip

The positioning of the hands on the club is important and most shots that swerve to the right or left can be attributed to a bad grip.

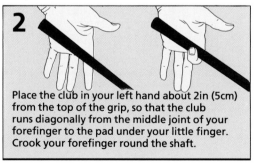

1 Feet together, extend your left arm comfortably, with the butt end of the club about 3 - 4in (7.5 - 10cm) from your left thigh.

2 Place the club in your left hand about 2in (5cm) from the top of the grip, so that the club runs diagonally from the middle joint of your forefinger to the pad under your little finger. Crook your forefinger round the shaft.

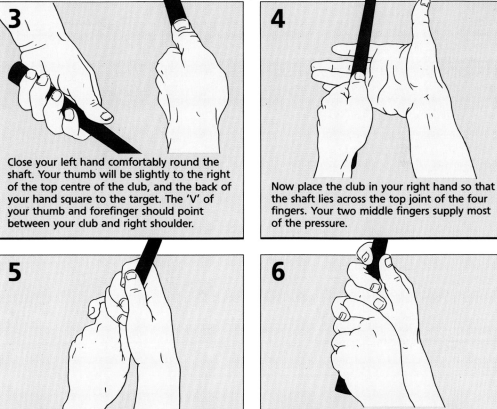

3

Close your left hand comfortably round the shaft. Your thumb will be slightly to the right of the top centre of the club, and the back of your hand square to the target. The 'V' of your thumb and forefinger should point between your club and right shoulder.

4

Now place the club in your right hand so that the shaft lies across the top joint of the four fingers. Your two middle fingers supply most of the pressure.

5

Close your fingers around the grip. The little finger overlaps the index finger of the left hand or, alternatively, you may prefer to place it in the cleft between the index and second fingers.

6

The completed grip. Note that your left thumb should not be stretched but rests naturally. When you've got it right, the back of your left hand, the front of your right and the club face will all be related and aimed squarely at the target.

NOTE: The pressure of your grip should only be firm enough to maintain control of the club – hold it too tightly and your swing will be badly affected.

Ball position

For every shot, the ball needs to be placed so that you can get a free swing at it. The position varies according to the club you are using, and there are two ways of getting this right. As a beginner, you will probably find the second method works better.

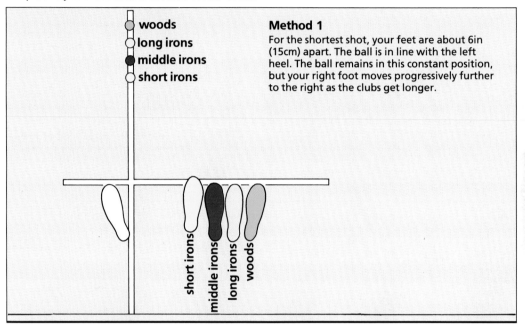

woods
long irons
middle irons
short irons

Method 1

For the shortest shot, your feet are about 6in (15cm) apart. The ball is in line with the left heel. The ball remains in this constant position, but your right foot moves progressively further to the right as the clubs get longer.

short irons
middle irons
long irons
woods

Method 2

Here the short shot is played with the ball placed half way between your heels. Again, start with your feet about 6in (15cm) apart.

For medium iron shots (numbers 5, 6 and 7), the ball is about 2in (5cm) to the right of your left heel.

For long iron and wood shots, place the ball opposite the left heel.

Stance and body alignment

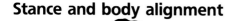

Imagine lines drawn across your toes and shoulders . . . should these point directly at your target? Many people playing golf might answer 'yes' but, in fact, this is not so. Better to imagine railway lines: the clubhead, ball and target on one side, and your shoulder and toe line on the other.

To get your stance right, have your left arm comfortably straight, the right arm slighty bent at the elbow. Imagine a line drawn between you and the ball and place your feet comfortably and firmly either side of this line, about 6-8in (15-20cm) apart.

Result: a perfect, square set-up with the lines across your toes, knees, hips, chest and shoulders all parallel to the ball-to-target line.

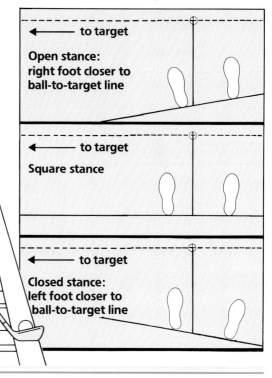

← to target

**Open stance:
right foot closer to
ball-to-target line**

← to target

Square stance

← to target

**Closed stance:
left foot closer to
ball-to-target line**

Posture

In order to swing the club in a fluid, co-ordinated movement, and in the correct plane (see page 28), it is important that you adopt the right posture when addressing the ball. But don't tense up. This should feel easy and natural with your body relaxed but not sloppy.

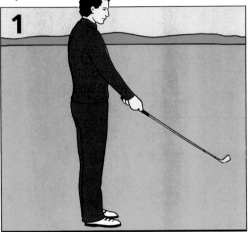

1 Stand upright with your legs straight, raising your arms and the club together until the clubhead is about 2ft (0.6m) off the ground.

2 Bend forward slightly from the hips, back held comfortably straight, until the base of your club is lying correctly on the ground. The amount you have to bend depends on the club you are using.

3 Now bend your knees forward and inward — not too much as this creates as much strain as straight legs. Your feet should be placed comfortably, with your weight evenly distributed.

The Backswing

This is the first part of the swing, bringing the club back and round ready to strike the ball. Think in terms of a winding up action, like pulling back a spring before releasing it. Keep your eyes on the back of the ball.

1

From the correct position of address, you will find a preliminary 'waggle' useful to get the feel of the club and the stroke needed. Don't move your shoulders for this, just your wrists.

2

At the start of the backswing, your hands, arms and club should move as one unit. Your left arm stays straight, and your shoulders will automatically start to turn. Your right hip will move slightly backwards in response. Remember you are bringing the club backwards as well as round.

3

At the top of the backswing, your shoulders should have turned 90°, your hips through 45°, and your left knee will have curved inwards (not forwards).

4

Your wrists are cocked so that the shaft is parallel to the ball-to-target line.

The Downswing

This, of course, is the phase of the swing in which you actually strike the ball.

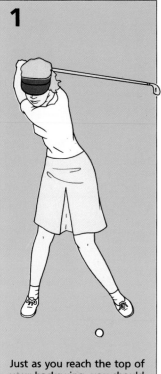

1

Just as you reach the top of your backswing, you should feel your left knee and left hand pulling leftwards to start the downswing.

2

A turning movement of the hips and shoulders swiftly follows, and automatically your arms and hands continue into the swing.

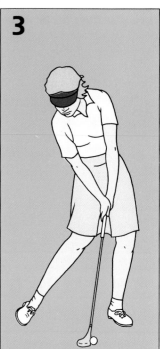

3

Think of the downswing as a powerful chain reaction, with your hips as the pivot. Imagine your shoulders and upper body conducting the power into your arms. Your arms multiply it and pass it into your hands, which in turn multiply the power still more. Note the position at impact.

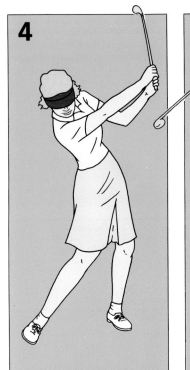

4

5

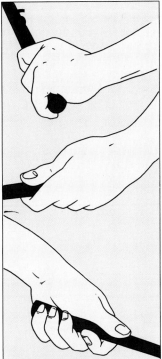

The released clubhead rushes powerfully through the air after impact. Note that the head is still behind the ball and eyes remain fixed on the ball's original position.

The momentum of the release carries the clubhead through and up. Your right arm should still be fully extended and your right knee will be bent in towards your left leg. Your head will automatically turn as you follow through.

Throughout the downswing, your wrists gradually supinate (rotate to face downwards) in preparation for striking the ball on time.

Plane

Imagine a pilot bringing an aircraft down. The angle of his descent must be neither too steep not too shallow if he's to hit the runway correctly. The angle at which your club approaches the ball before and during impact is also an important factor in a successful swing. This angle – made by your clubhead's path (or arc) in relation to the ground – is known as the plane of your swing. Remember: incorrect posture (see page 24) will adversely affect your plane.

Correct plane

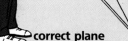

correct plane

Imagine a line drawn from your shoulder to the centre of the ball and try to keep this line the same throughout the swing. Many golf tutors suggest an imaginary pane of glass resting on your shoulders. From hip-level upwards your clubhead stays parallel to, and just underneath, the glass.

Alternative planes

steep plane   **shallow plane**

The plane will vary according to the club you are using – the shorter the club, the steeper the plane. Your height also affects the plane – if you are tall your plane will be steeper (or more upright) than a shorter person's.

Deciding Which Club to Use

How do you decide which club to use? To a beginner this is one of the most baffling elements of golf. You have probably heard the terms 'underclub' and 'overclub' or the instruction to 'use more club' or 'use less club' ('more club' means a club with less loft, which gives you more distance). The fact is that each stroke needs to be considered for its own particular requirements, and this will come only with practice. However, the following guidelines may help you speed up the process!

Distance

It is a good idea to find out on the practice ground how far you can hit the ball with each of your clubs. Using a 6- or 7-iron, hit a dozen practice balls on flat ground and measure the distance (by counting your paces) to the middle of the group of balls. Then you can easily work out your likely distance for the other clubs by adding or subtracting 10-12yds (9-11m) for each.

The tables opposite give very approximate distances for the different clubs, based on an average male player hitting in reasonable conditions.

Other factors

Different situations – the slope of the ground, for example – will require you to use more or less club than the distance alone would suggest (see page 38). When playing a course, the 'course planner', if available, can be very helpful since it illustrates features as well as distances.

Woods	Approximate distance
No 1	245yds (224m)
No 3	225yds (205m)
No 5	205yds (187m)

Irons	Approximate distance
2-iron	190yds (174m)
3-iron	180yds (165m)
4-iron	170yds (155m)
5-iron	160yds (146m)
6-iron	150yds (137m)
7-iron	140yds (128m)
8-iron	130yds (119m)
9-iron	120yds (110m)
Pitching wedge	100yds (91m)
Sand-iron	80yds (73m)

Short Iron Shots

These are the high shots made with numbers 6-, 7-, 8- and 9-irons and the wedge and sand-iron. They are used for shots 130yds (119m) or less from the hole. These are precision shots and there is no substitute for practice!

   NOTE: All instructions below, and on the following pages, are for right-handed players. If you are left-handed, reverse the instructions as appropriate.

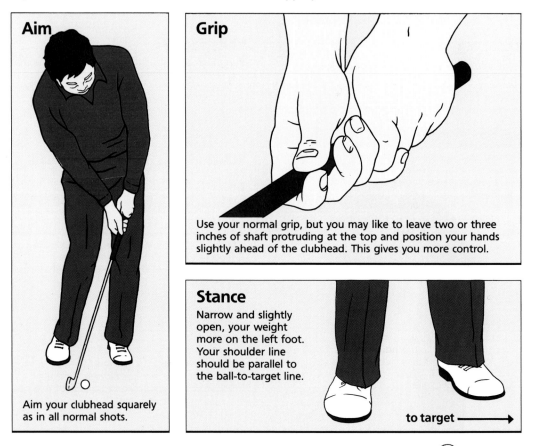

Aim

Aim your clubhead squarely as in all normal shots.

Grip

Use your normal grip, but you may like to leave two or three inches of shaft protruding at the top and position your hands slightly ahead of the clubhead. This gives you more control.

Stance

Narrow and slightly open, your weight more on the left foot. Your shoulder line should be parallel to the ball-to-target line.

to target ⟶

The chip

This is a low-running approach shot usually played with a 6- or 7-iron. Use it around the green if there are no obstacles. You don't need much backswing, and should keep your wrist action to an absolute minimum.

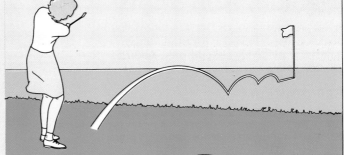

The pitch

A high-dropping shot with very little run on it played with a pitching wedge or sand-iron. Use it to pitch the ball close to the hole. Cock your wrists early to create a steep, narrow backswing and try to hit down and through the ball to create maximum backspin and therefore minimum run.

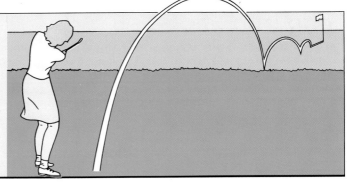

Pitch and run

Here you aim to get the ball down sooner and continue an accurate path after landing. In fact, a third of the total shot will run along the ground. This is often more effective than a pitch since it is easier to predict run than flight. Cock your wrists less for this shot.

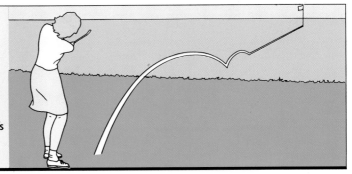

Medium Iron Shots

When you want to hit the ball a reasonable distance, use a 5-, 6- or 7-iron, all clubs which are relatively easy to play. Address the ball in the usual way.

Ball position

Imagine a line drawn from the inside of your left heel to the ball-to-target line and position the ball about 2in (5cm) right of this line. This helps with height and backspin.

Long Iron Shots

The 2-, 3- and 4-irons are probably the hardest for a beginner or average player because of their long length and lack of loft. You'll need regular practice to develop good technique. It is tempting to hit the ball harder simply because the shot is longer but, remember, you should apply the same pace of swing as you would to a 6- or 7-iron. Address the ball in the normal way but note the following points:

Grip

Check your grip pressure. With a long-iron shot you may be tempted to hold too tightly because of the length of the shot.

Ball position

Play the ball from a point opposite your left heel and strike it with a square, accelerating clubface.

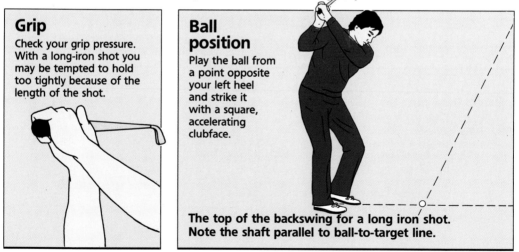

The top of the backswing for a long iron shot. Note the shaft parallel to ball-to-target line.

Fairway Woods

Inexperienced players are often nervous of playing a wood when it's not on a tee. It is really a matter of practice and gaining confidence. The basic swing remains the same; the ball position is the most important point to note.

1 Place the ball in line with a spot 1½-2in (3.8-5cm) to the right of your left heel.

2 Don't try to hit too hard, or grip the club too tightly.

3 Practise from a low tee at first, then progress to a smooth bit of turf as your confidence increases.

4 Start with your most lofted wood and gradually drop down to a number 4 or number 3.

5 Once you can hit reasonably accurately from good lies, try a downslope or tight bare lie. You will need a steeper attack, which gives the ball a left-to-right spin, so aim left of your target.

Completion of a full drive. Note the smooth, balanced finish.

Putting

The importance of putting consistently round the greens cannot be over-emphasised. This is where good scores are made or lost, and plenty of practice is required.

Aim

First check the line from behind the ball. Then sole the putter directly behind the ball, with the face at right angles to the target line.

Grip

Many golfers adjust their grip for putting. The most commonly used grip is the reverse overlap – as described on page 21 but with the index finger of the left hand overlapping the little finger of the right.

Posture, stance and ball position

It is important to keep your body still and relaxed throughout the shot. Even turning your shoulders slightly can pull your putt blade off-line. So when addressing the ball, concentrate on building maximum stability into your set-up.

NOTE: The putter should always hit the ball and never scuff the ground – this will lead to an erratic stroke.

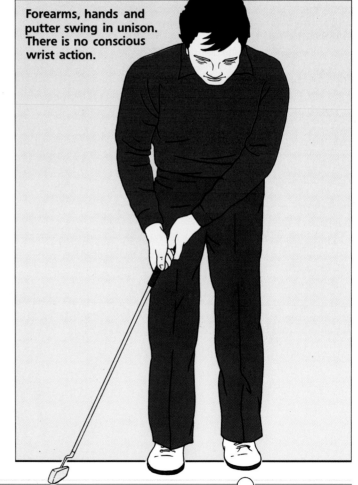

Forearms, hands and putter swing in unison. There is no conscious wrist action.

Read the green

Most greens are not completely flat and you will need to aim to the left or right to allow for the ball to divert according to any sideslope. The amount you need to allow is called the 'borrow'. The line you choose also depends on how fast you intend to hit the putt: the harder you hit, the less the ball will break.

Reading the green in this way is a matter of feel and comes with experience and practice (see page 46).

Here the putter head is aimed to the right of the hole to allow for about 2ft (0.6m) of right-to-left borrow.

Get the distance right

On long putts, first take into account any slope, then pick a spot to aim at. Set up to that spot and look at it, but then almost forget it in terms of direction and concentrate instead on the distance. You are unlikely to get more than a couple of feet off-line but distance is much harder to get right. It may help to imagine a target with a 4ft (1.22m) diameter around the hole.

Bunker Shots

Even the most accurate golfer will sometimes face the prospect of playing from the sand, but with practice this need not hold any fears.

Greenside bunkers

There's no harm in aiming to hole the ball – good golfers can sometimes do it – but your first consideration is to escape from the sand.

Using your sand-iron, adopt an open stance and position the ball just inside your left heel. Your clubface should be square or slightly open to the flagstick. The swingpath is parallel to your feet. Your target is the sand, not the ball: aim about 1½-2in (3.8-5cm) behind the ball, which will pop up as the displaced sand explodes it into the air. Imagine the ball as an egg you're not allowed to break!

Fairway bunkers

Here you need distance as well as height, but make sure you choose a club which will give you enough height to clear the lip of the hazard. A 5-, 6- or 7-iron is usually best.

Position the ball midway between your feet. Your club face should be square to the target line, and your hands just forward of the ball at address. Firm up your grip a little and keep your eye on the top of the ball. Aim to hit the back of the ball – if you clip sand first, the shot will be dead.

What do you do if . . .

. . . the sand is sparse or hard after rain?
Use a 9-iron instead of your sand-iron but play the shot with a slightly open club to give extra loft.

. . . the ball is plugged?
If the ball is embedded in the sand, use a sand-iron or pitching wedge and close the club face slightly. Aim one and half to two inches behind the ball. Because there is no backspin, allow for the ball to run freely on landing.

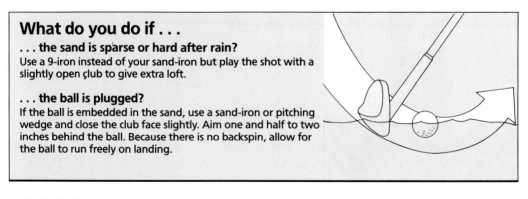

Bunker shots – uphill slope

When you are tackling a sloping lie in a bunker, don't try to keep your usual vertical stance. Lean with the slope, with your weight mainly on your right foot and your left leg bent. Position the ball left of centre. Then play your normal shot, with the swing parallel to the sand surface.

Bunker shots – downhill slope

Again, adjust your stance to go with the slope, this time with your weight mainly on your left foot and your right leg bent.

Remember that your club must not touch the ball or the sand before you strike (see page 18 No. 2). Penalty: two strokes.

Awkward Lies

The description of the swing on pages 20-28 assumes that you want to hit a straight shot from a flat lie. Since real life is not always like that, here are some hints on how to adapt the basics to suit prevailing conditions.

Uphill lie
- Take more club (see page 29), typically one or two less lofted than the distance suggests.
- Aim right because the ball will travel to the left (hook) during flight.
- Keep your shoulders parallel to the ground.
- Keep your head steady.

Downhill lie
- Take less club (see page 29).
- Aim left because the ball will travel right (slice) in flight.
- Position the ball in front of your higher foot.
- Bend your right knee more and tilt into the slope.

Sideways lie – ball above feet
- Position the ball midway between your feet.
- Grip the club lower down and play the shot mainly with hands and arms.
- Adopt a more upright position.
- Aim right to allow for ball hooking in flight.

Sideways lie – ball below feet
- Position the ball towards your left foot.
- Grip the club closer to the top.
- Bend your knees more than usual.
- Aim left to allow for ball slicing in flight.

Deliberate Slicing and Hooking

Being able to get the ball to travel with a directional spin can be a useful skill in a variety of situations — if there's a wind to combat, for example, or when you need to swerve round some trees. These shots depend on the alignment of the clubface at impact; they are skilled shots needing practice.

Hooking

Here the ball travels in a right-to-left direction. Position the ball in line with a point 2-3in (5-7.6cm) to the right of your left heel. Your stance is slighty closed so that your footline points slightly to the right of the target or obstacle, but your clubface aims straight at the target following an in-to-out path.

A shot with a very slight right-to-left flight is known as a draw.

Slicing

This is a shot which travels left and then slices to the right because of the spin put on it. To achieve it, position the ball in line with your left heel. Open your stance so that your feet and shoulders are pointing left of the target or obstacle, but aim your clubface straight at the target. This will encourage an out-to-in swingpath and the ball will spin rightwards as it climbs.

The degree of slicing depends on how much you open your stance. A shot with a very slight left-to-right flight is known as a fade.

NOTE: A ball hit from left to right will tend to stop quickly after landing; a ball hit from right to left will run on after landing.

Correcting Faults

These are the common errors which everyone — even top professionals — will encounter at some time. If you find you are making mistakes, always check through the basics of address first, particularly grip, ball position and stance.

Slicing

Whilst there are occasions which call for the deliberate use of the slice (see page 39), you will find that the ball sometimes moves from left to right in error, losing length and causing trouble.

Cause:
- Clubhead too open to the swingpath at impact; swingpath excessively out-to-in.

Check that:
- Your grip is not too weak, with one or both hands twisted too far to the left — this would make it hard to return the club squarely to the ball at impact.
- You are not starting the downswing with your shoulders, making the clubhead 'chop' across the target line and keeping your weight too much on your right side.
- The ball is not too far to the left causing an open set-up.

Hooking

Here the ball moves sideways from right to left instead of straight to target, again losing the shot's accuracy.

Cause:
- Clubface too closed to the swingpath at impact; swingpath excessively in-to-out.

Check that:
- Your grip is not too strong, with hands twisted too far to the right — this would give a closed clubface at impact.
- Your swing is wide and deep enough, following through inside the target line.
- The ball is not positioned too far right.
- Your hips are turning naturally through impact.

Pulling

The pull is a shot that flies straight but left of the target.

Cause:
- An out-to-in swing. Your clubface points left of the target.

Check that:
- Your stance and alignment are not aimed too much to the left.
- The ball is not too far forward.
- Your arms and left knee start the backswing.
- You are not taking the club back too much on the inside and then looping it to the outside when you start the downswing.

Pushing

A push is the exact opposite of a pull, with the ball travelling straight through the air but to the right of target.

Cause:
- An in-to-out swing. Your clubface points right of the target.

Check that:
- Your stance and alignment are not aimed too much to the right.
- The ball is not too far back.
- You are not swaying towards the target during the downswing and impact.

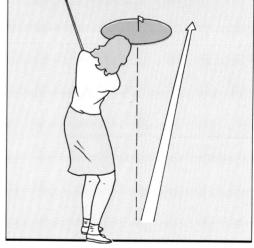

If you find yourself consistently pushing or pulling, a useful aid is to concentrate on the actual impact. As you start the backswing, make sure the club travels straight back from the ball for 10-12in (25-30cm). Then, on the downswing, concentrate on retracing this path to strike the ball squarely along that line.

Overswinging
Cause:
- This is as it sounds: taking the swing back too far so that at the top of the backswing the club has gone beyond horizontal. This results in loss of control of your clubhead.

Check that:
- Your grip pressure at address is correct.
- Your elbows are flexed inwards at address and your weight is evenly distributed.
- You are not rolling the clubface open as you start the backswing.
- Your left arm isn't buckling at the top of the backswing.
- You are not lifting your left heel too much.

Topping
Here the bottom edge of your club strikes the middle or upper part of the ball, severely restricting its distance and often damaging the ball.

Cause:
- Usually an incorrect position at address resulting in an out-to-in swingpath with your weight staying on your back foot.

Check that:
- The ball is not too far away at address.
- You are not holding your breath, or holding the club too tightly, causing tension.
- You don't move your head up at impact.
- Your knees are properly flexed.

NOTE: As with all the common errors, do check through all the basics of address first.

Fluffing

This is the infuriating shot where the club hits the ground before contacting the ball, robbing the shot of much of its length. At its worst it results in an enormous divot with the ball travelling just a few feet.

Cause:
- Usually an incorrect set-up: run through the basics first.

Check that:
- Your head is held steady throughout the swing.
- You are not standing too close to the ball.
- You are not crouching too much.
- Your swing is steep enough and your weight-shift from right to left is complete.

Shanking

The part of the club where the shaft meets the blade is called the hosel. In a shank, the hosel strikes the ball, causing it to spin violently to the right. This shot is also known as a socket.

Cause:
- Swinging your clubhead in a plane that is too flat or too steep; an in-to-out swing.

Check that:
- Your hands don't move too far away from your body and your elbows are held in.
- The ball is not too far forward or back.
- Your stance is not too open or too closed.
- Your left knee doesn't turn outwards on the backswing making your right knee tighten.

Preparation

All pros warm up and practise before playing and it is even more important for beginners and average players to do so. This is where you will fine-tune your game, working on weaker points. The right kind of practice will do wonders for the consistency of your game.

Warm-up

Warming up is a vital preparation for any sport, and golf is no exception. Any general stretching is good, particularly for arms, hands and legs, but here are a couple of simple warm-ups to get you started. Never overstretch – do them gently.

1 Twisting. Hook a club behind your back between your arms and, with feet comfortably apart, twist your hips and body as far as you can to the right. Hold for a count of 10, then repeat to the left. Repeat twice more to each side.

2 Club swings. Hold two long-iron clubs at once and practise a few gentle swings, back and forth in a smooth, continuous action. Repeat 10 times.

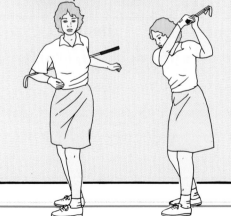

Some general points

1 Practise your weakest shots most, aiming to transform them into the strongest part of your game – a great confidence builder.

2 If you are getting stuck and not making progress in a part of your game, have a few lessons with a pro.

3 Concentrate most on your short game, especially putting.

4 Practise as often as you can. A little and often, if possible, is better than one longer session. You can always use your lawn or a nearby park for short shots!

On the Practice Ground

1 For building up confidence in actually striking the ball, use a pitching wedge or 9-iron and aim at a target. Strike about 25-30 balls one at a time, then go and collect them and assess your accuracy.

2 Practise hitting from different lies. Try to imagine different course situations and practise appropriate shots – for example, imagine you are striking against a strong right-to-left cross wind and aim slightly right.

3 Remember that when you are practising long shots, accuracy of direction is what you are aiming for; with short shots, length is the more difficult aspect to master. Set your practice targets accordingly.

4 Practise hitting shots with your heels together. This helps your timing and balance.

Course management

Being able to recognise and make the most of your current abilities is what course management is all about. This means looking at each hole from the tee to the green and not always trying to go straight towards the flag. Look for the easiest rather than the quickest route and always aim to get onto the green in a direction that gives you the simplest putt – uphill if possible.

Putting Practice

The importance of practising your short game, particularly putting, has already been emphasised. Being a good putter is probably the best confidence-builder of all.

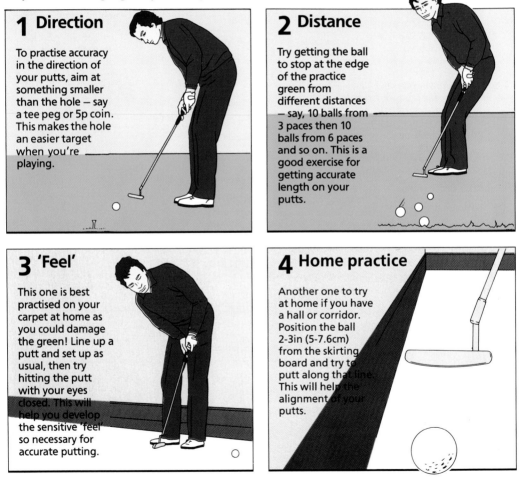

1 Direction

To practise accuracy in the direction of your putts, aim at something smaller than the hole — say a tee peg or 5p coin. This makes the hole an easier target when you're playing.

2 Distance

Try getting the ball to stop at the edge of the practice green from different distances — say, 10 balls from 3 paces then 10 balls from 6 paces and so on. This is a good exercise for getting accurate length on your putts.

3 'Feel'

This one is best practised on your carpet at home as you could damage the green! Line up a putt and set up as usual, then try hitting the putt with your eyes closed. This will help you develop the sensitive 'feel' so necessary for accurate putting.

4 Home practice

Another one to try at home if you have a hall or corridor. Position the ball 2-3in (5-7.6cm) from the skirting board and try to putt along that line. This will help the alignment of your putts.

Glossary

ADDRESS	The player's position in relation to the ball before making the swing.
ANGLE OF ATTACK	The angle at which the clubhead approaches the ball on the downswing.
APPROACH SHOT	Any shot towards the green from about 150yds (137m) inwards.
BIRDIE	A score of one stroke under par for a hole.
BOGEY	A score of one stroke over par for a hole.
BORROW	The amount to allow for the ball to deviate on a sideways slope.
CHIP	A low-running approach shot.
CLOSED ALIGNMENT	When the left side of the body is closer to the ball-to-target line than the right.
CLOSED FACE	Clubface aimed left of the correct position.
CLOSED STANCE	When the left foot is closer to the target line than the right.
CLUBFACE	The club's striking surface.
DIVOT	Piece of turf disturbed by the club.
DORMIE	When a player or team is ahead in a match by as many holes as there are left to play.

DRAW	A ball with a slight right-to-left curve through the air.
DRIVE	A shot played from the teeing ground with a number 1 wood.
EAGLE	A score of two strokes under par for a hole.
FADE	A ball with a slight left-to-right curve through the air.
FOLLOW-THROUGH	A part of the swing after impact.
HANDICAP	A player's scoring ability against the standard scratch score of a course.
HOOK	A shot which curves from right to left.
HOSEL	The part of the club where the shaft meets the clubface.
IN-TO-OUT	The clubhead travelling from inside the ball-to-target line to outside it through the swing.
LESS CLUB	A higher-numbered club with more loft giving less distance.
LIE	The angle formed by the sole of the club with the shaft. Also used to describe the position of the ball.
MORE CLUB	A lower-numbered club with less loft giving more distance.

OPEN FACE — Clubface aimed right of the correct position.

OPEN STANCE — When the right foot is closer to the target line than the left.

OUT OF BOUNDS — Outside the course, whose boundaries are marked by fences, ditches or trees.

OUT-TO-IN — The clubhead travelling from outside the ball-to-target line to inside it through the swing.

OVERCLUB — Use of a low-numbered club with insufficient loft and too much distance.

PAR — The score expected by a first-class player for a hole, allowing two strokes on the green.

PITCH — A high approach shot.

PLUGGED — A ball stuck in its own indentation in soft ground or sand.

PULL — A shot which travels straight but to the left of target.

PUSH — A shot which travels straight but to the right of target.

SCRATCH SCORE — The standard score for a course against which handicaps are allocated.

SHANK — A shot struck by the hosel, also known as a SOCKET.

SLICE — A shot which curves from left to right.

SOCKET — See SHANK.

SOLE (verb) — To rest the base of the club on the ground.

SQUARE STANCE — With both feet the same distance from the ball-to-target line.

TARGET LINE — The line connecting the ball with the target.

TIGHT BARE LIE — Describes a ball positioned where grass is sparse or very short.

TOP — An error shot where the ball is struck above its equator.

UNDERCLUB — Use of a high-numbered club with too much loft and insufficient distance.

WAGGLE — A smooth back-and-forth wrist movement preceding the swing.